Where the Oil Went

SAVANAH JUDD

WHERE THE OIL WENT

Copyright © 2020 Savanah Judd
All rights reserved.
ISBN: 979-8-6307-1734-4

PREFACE

What lie on the pages of this book are not bougie attempts at intellectualism or some poser form of depth. I am a creative. Not for the sake of art or showmanship, but because I have the ability to create new worlds within me and the answer to the world around me is the world within me.

What I write doesn't require a stance and quite frankly isn't designed for one. My desire is to bring about mature, abstract thinking, in which I believe every individual holds the ability to perform. My desire is to stir the waters of passion and ignite the fire of contemplation. Being still and listening is the most underrated concept in all of history. If we would simply slow our pace and open our ears, the mysteries of the universe just might begin to open up. One may even begin to hear the groans of creation. And as scary as it may seem, one may even begin to hear their own inner voice and possibly the voice that formed creation itself and has been trying to speak to it ever since.

Before we rummage through my anthology of letters and words and feelings that I am somewhat scared of, yet all too excited to share with you, I would like to honor every person that is reading this. Not because that is what an author should feel obligated to do, but because from the very innermost part of my being I would find it necessary to honor every eye that skims the pages of this book, every action you went through to possess this work, and most of all your time.

~ **Savanah Judd**

INTRODUCTION

I believe that as I was writing these poems long ago, I was prophesying a redemptive journey of the generations. These words came from prayers, visions, dreams, encounters, and intercession. They came from the inner man in me that cried out for freedom & righteousness and for the nearing generations to come alive. The will of God is man fully alive and with every poem I wrote, it felt as though I was composing a symphony that would shake the chambers within the heart of God's people. I didn't want to stop with mere shaking, so I went low until I found the deepest desire of our soul, and that is to be touched.

I wanted to tell you the story of how I got to where I am and every harsh detail of my experiences, but I don't think that is what I want to share now. That part of my story is now something that me and Father share. It's one of those things that tie us together, that I can look back on and feel held. I want to give you my journey to healing, wholeness, redemption, restoration, and peace. I want to do this because mercy triumphs over judgement and because our creator is a trader. Joy for mourning, a garment of praise for our heaviness, and beauty for ashes. I want to share a story with you that chooses life instead of death...

WHERE THE OIL WENT

i am a prostitute.
or at least... i was.
or maybe i was
prostituted.

i lured them in with
eloquent words,
passionate poetry, and
holy whispers.
the system labeled it
"evangelism".

they saw the smallest bit
of hunger.
desire.
gifting.
"Let's sell it."

they renamed me with
titles i didn't even want.
turn me into a model used
for advertising.
i may have been seen as
pure,
but that's not what i felt
like when i almost
collapsed under the
pressure of
performance.

give them what they want.
meet their expectations.
and make sure not to let
them down.

my body was passed
around,
made where everyone
could see,
and then sent off.

they may have been
willing to pay the price,
but what about an
investment?

"network so you can
expand."
but this only led to me
getting into bed with
a "yes"
that gave consent to an
inferior intimacy.

it looked good. i know it
did.
i was the porn, providing
unrealistic expectations
for anyone who would
watch.

i extorted the truth only to
create a brothel of
spectators.

they called me Godly,
angelic, holy...
"on fire" was my favorite,
but it wasn't until I was
actually exposed to it,
that it burnt up the whore
house within me.

i traded my wander for
wonder.

my houses for a home.
one-night stands for
relationship.
rags for a robe.
i discovered love for the
first time.
one man. one bride.
"I do."

- *"Whore"*

{inspired by the Song of Solomon}

He's put the runner back in me,
fueled by a source of intimacy.
He's brought me into His bedroom.
i should be focused on eyes filled with wonder and wisdom.
instead the precarious thoughts of insecurity come back.
i am dark...but lovely.

I begin to find resentment in the ones that were supposed to love me.
they were angry! They forced me!
I am marked now!
i can't hide it!
dark, but lovely.

but my own vineyard; it's untouched, it's uncared for, it's neglected.
where are you going today?
i don't want to be like the wandering prostitute.
i just want home.

there you are on your couch again, enchanted by my perfume.
but how can it be so captivating if i have yet to pour it out?
maybe its proximity.

left arm under my head.
right arm around me.
have i become numb to the embrace?

i can hear it!
"Come away!"
"Come away!"
"Come away with me!"
You beg.
You honor me and i am learning to honor You.
my lover is mine and i am His.

i lay here yearning for You.
I get up and ravage the city to come find You.
You are worth it.
after the pursuit i finally find you.
i take you back to the beginning where predestined intimacy was first conceived.

You tell me i have captured your heart.

You call me your treasure,
your bride.
that makes you more than
master.
we share a private garden.

the intruders have beat me
and bruised me.
they stripped me of my
covering.
turn my veil into a sail.
i can go anywhere.
i'm not going anywhere.
only back to the garden.

You lure me into the
wilderness.

You transform me.
the ones that were supposed
to love me have showed up
again.
they don't recognize me,
but that's okay.
all i say is i belong to Him.
my vineyard is mine and
mine to give.

- *"The Shulamite"*

olive.
the complexion of a passionate lover.
the fruits which are strategically placed outside the plantations of the beautiful, plump origins of what will soon become the delightful spirits that will dance on the lips of the people.

olive.
so small and insignificant, yet the byproduct flows from a fountain of purpose.
used for extravagance.
healing.
anointing.
burial.
nourishment.
provision.
fuel.

this oil, i will not receive by prostitution.
i will not be fenced in by thorn bushes.
no. I will receive it by running through the fields, gathering the fruits of the harvest.
only to watch them be pressed into a fiery fuel source, in which i will cover myself.
no. i am not afraid of the burning.
not afraid of the marks that will be left.
because my lover says that although I am dark, I am lovely.

lovely, yes, lovely.
this oil.
it will soften my skin.
my heart.
making me presentable before my king.
only in hopes for intimacy.

- *"Oil"*

SAVANAH JUDD

it's the first thing we
never had to learn to do.
someone else did it for us.
He came down low.
got on our level.
got messy.

face to face.
mouth to mouth.
it was given to us.
breath.
it was ours.

step one - inhale.
step two - exhale.
breathe.

for the first time in years,
i can do this simple act.
let me rephrase.
it doesn't hurt anymore.

the pressure's off.
The weight was ripped
out of me.
the wine of healing is
being poured out and i am
overfilling.

did you hear me?
the pressure's off!!
no more expectations.
no more striving.
no more incorrect
identities.

i stopped running because
i found home.
"Welcome home!"
where it's okay to be
seated and be.
just be.

it was in the arms
of the most unexpected
man
that i discovered this.

i tried to resist. i really
did.
i still remember it. you
know what i mean.
when the only thing you
have left is the lump in
your throat.

"Relax. Catch your
breath. Just breathe."

- *"Breath"*

SAVANAH JUDD

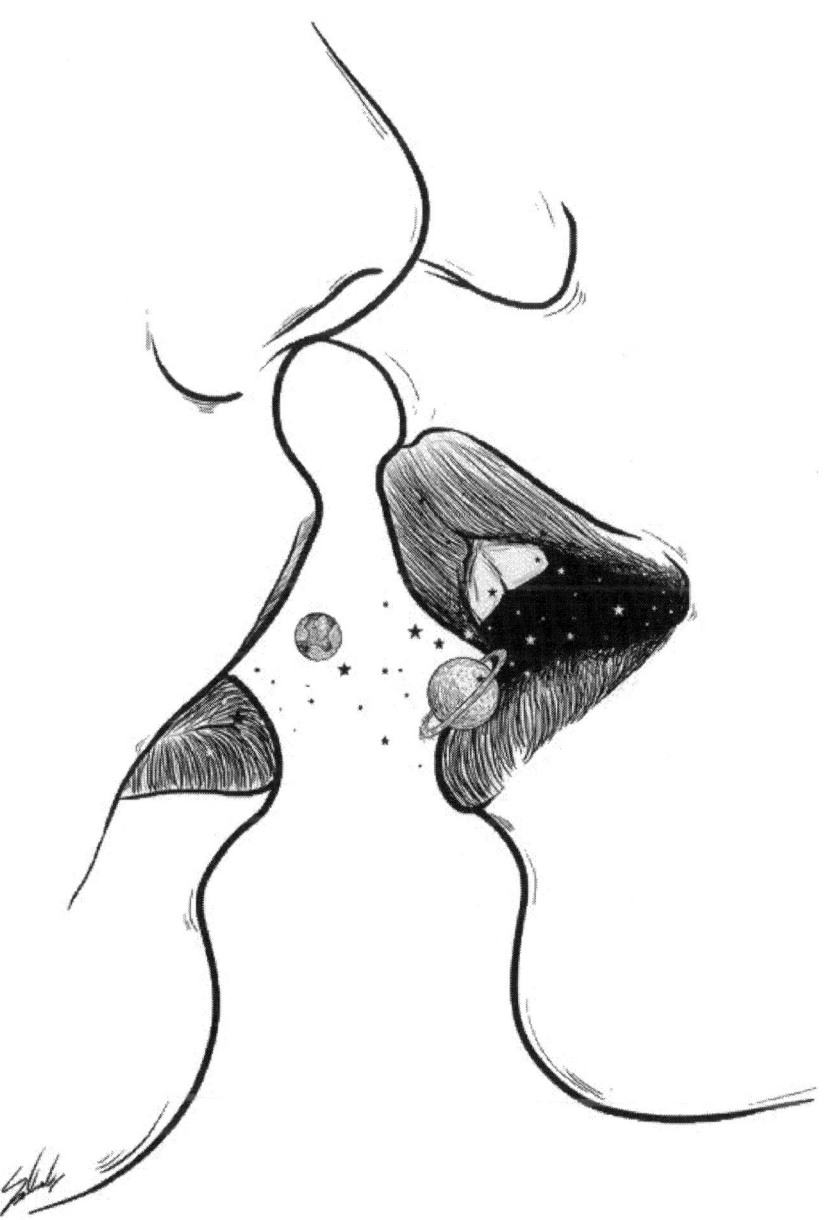

ishmael.
the byproduct of an
inferior intimacy.
the aftermath of an
impatience that couldn't
wait for the promise.

unplanned? no.
compromised.
incorrect.
insufficient.

all he had to do was say,
"Yes".
to intimacy.
to honor.
to chasing sarah around
the tent.

isn't it what we do,
though?
we conceive inadequate
mindsets that tell us we
have to help God fulfill
what He's promised.

we turn vision into a goal.
we turn vision into
humanistic goal
orientation.
we turn inheritance into
work.

we were designed to carry
legacy.
we were designed for a
lineage.
we were designed to
reproduce an image that
would reflect into
generations.

look up.
do you see the
descendants?
there's too many to count.
that's the reflection He
was talking about.

i will not be in bed with
anymore Hagars.
it wasn't the plan.
it still isn't.
i will wait on my Isaac.

- *"Ishmael"*

SAVANAH JUDD

we have been taught
and trained
and drilled
and screamed at.
"Be a good soldier!"

fight hard.
be prepared.
the war is all around us.
don't die. be okay.

the system has tried to train
us up.
this is how you war.
hand to hand combat. day
after day.
scream a little louder,
the enemy can't hear you.

suit up.
put on the armor.
don't let your guard down.
don't die.

we have somehow come
under the impression that
victory
is dripping sweat
stomping feet
and mutilated vocal cords
from our empty shouts.

"Name the spirit."
like it's a game show.

chase it down, hunt it out,
and attack.
who looks more like the
enemy now?

no! i refuse to live life at
war.
demonic fascination is not
my hobby.
i will not exalt the enemy
more than the king.
i will release air strikes,
because generals are
soldiers too.
they just know where
they're seated.
positioned up high.

WHY!! WHY!!
why can't I be like David?
he didn't want the weight of
other people's inferior
protection holding him
back.
he didn't battle
like you and me.
he just played his harp and
watched the demons flee.

his warfare was like
worship.
his warfare was worship.

- *"Redefining Warfare"*

SAVANAH JUDD

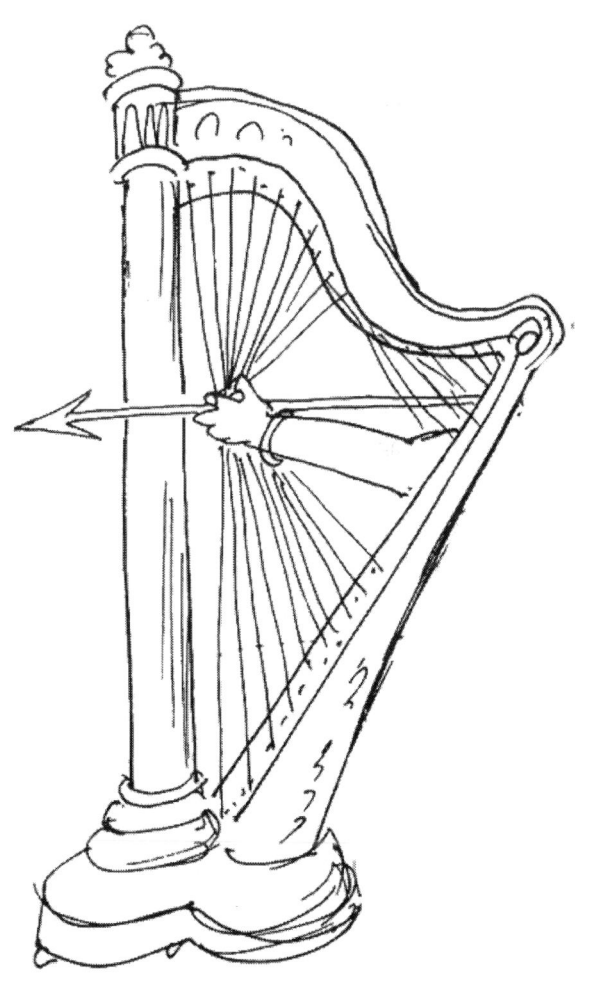

oh, woman of the streets,
they don't understand.
you are bold. You are sure.
you are unapologetic.

that day you entered
Simon's home.
you weren't quite welcome,
but you also weren't
banished.
those jews seemed to know
who you were.
almost as if they were
familiar with you.

they seemed to know you so
well that they questioned
the Christ.
"do you not know who this
woman is?"

oh, woman of the streets,
you are extravagant.
you are forever honored in
history.
your worship.
it was not correct.
it was not dignified.
it was not pretty.
it was uncompromised.

your worship was worth
more than any debt a man
could owe.
worth more than the
alabaster box you carry.

you finally found the man
who didn't want anything
from you.
yet, you gave it all anyway.

your tears as honored
just as much as your
perfume
and your kisses
just as much as the
cleansing.

your oil was not wasted.
don't let them tell you any
different.
they can't take away the
scent
that will forever tie you to
your beloved.

- **"Extravagance"**

SAVANAH JUDD

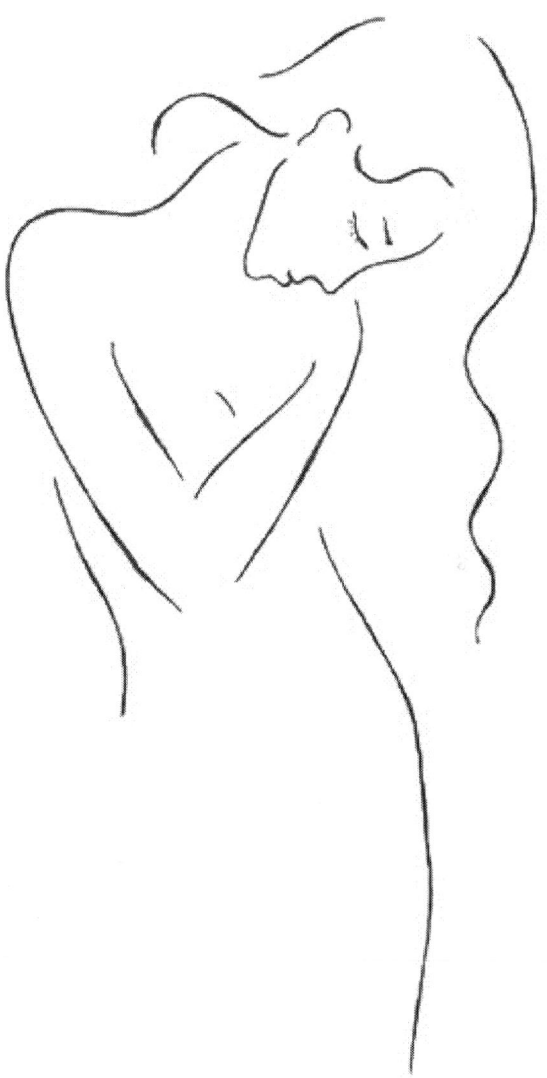

i looked at the ground.
she was trying to make her own way.
beloved, why don't you walk in the path
that has already been made?

sink deep into the footprints of the Father.
he went ahead for a reason.
step out of the striving.
there's no fear of falling here.

- *"Watch Your Step"*

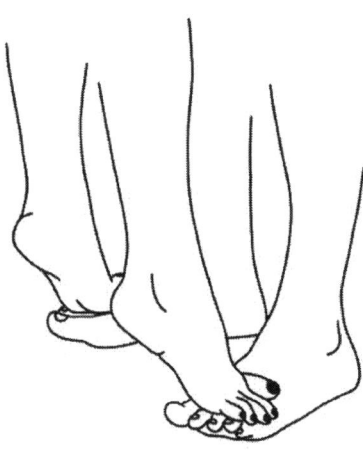

i remember our first
dance.
when i fell into Your
arms.
that's when i found home.

home wasn't what i
expected.
it was oddly familiar.
yet, I've never known
anything like it.

i catch glimpses of Your
face.
Your eyes.
they are blazing.
like the flames of the
campfires you use to woo
me into the night.

i am pursuing the promise
of the ascended life.
the awakened bride.

i am my beloved's and
He is mine.
we are in no hurry.
here time is irrelevant.
that's why we slow
dance.

- **"*Slow Dance*"**

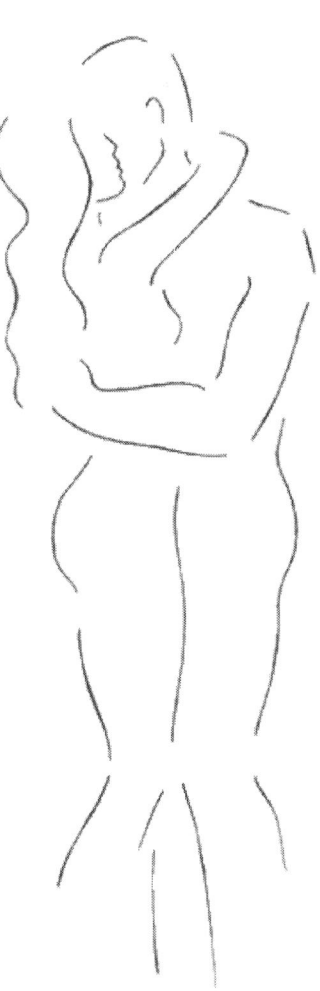

i am still.
i can feel my chest rising
and falling.
i am breathing.
involuntarily engaging
with an invisible life
source.

i am still.
it's easy to tame the noise
of outside forces.
it's sound from the
internal world that i am
learning the art of
quieting.

i am still.
re-familiarizing my
senses with the elements
of home.
finding joy in the
discovery of
another realm.
one for which i am
returning to.

you see,
things are not new.
it's just the remembering
of what was.

here are the directions:
sit down.
your name is beloved,
not pioneer.

i am here.
i am awake.
i am present.
full of life.
i am still.

- *"I Am Still"*

SAVANAH JUDD

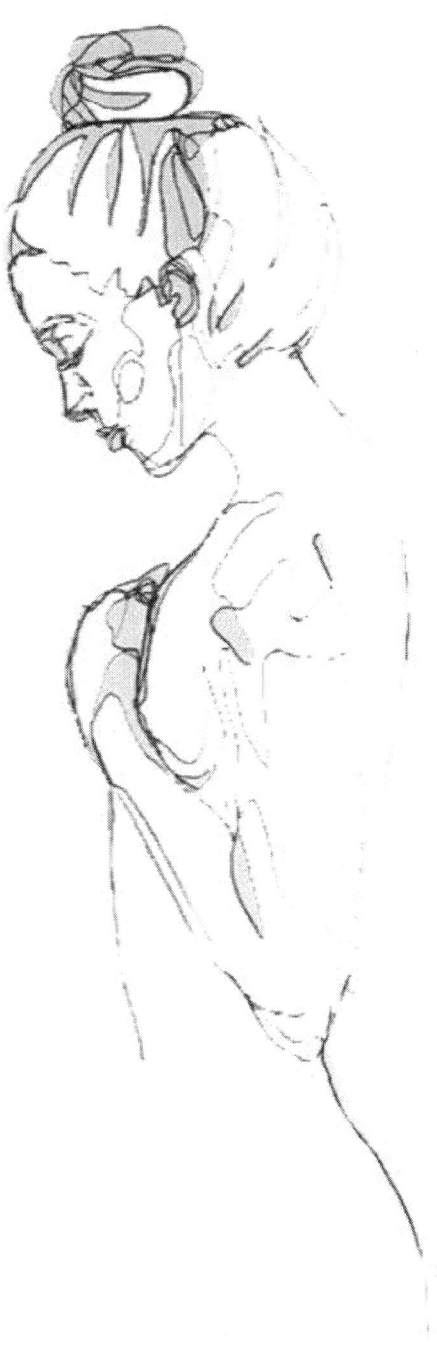

we can only dream of
what we have already
seen.
or at least that's what
they say.
i believe that is only
denial
rejecting the possibility of
wonder.

i dream of another world.
of another dimension.
one that does not even
compare to this current
captivity.

i dream of the
unthinkable.
the things that have not
yet been seen
or heard
or even imagined.

i dream of what has yet to
come
or maybe of the before.

or maybe they're right.
we can only dream of
what we have seen.
that's why it's no longer
me.
no longer my mind.
no longer my eyes.

i am one with another.
One who has seen it all.
One who can create and
make and form and build
and construct the most
glorious imagery that
goes beyond humanistic
boundaries.
we try to say it's the
unseen.

but you see, the unseen, it
isn't so far away.

- *"Unseen Dreams"*

SAVANAH JUDD

Come Away!
Come Away!
Come Away!
You beg.

You are wooing your
bride deep into the night.
guiding her by the
campfires in your eyes.

they are blazing.
i have been marked by
your flames.
yes, I have been
"sun kissed".
dark, but lovely.

unveil yourself, Beloved.
the only way to get close
is to get close.
let's get face to face.
you were designed for
intimacy from the very
first day.

but you see, love at first
sight doesn't have to be
reciprocated in order to
be valid.

I saw you first.
I knew you before the
beginning.
before there was.

that's why it's illegal to
only trust what you can
see.
I have things hidden in
My heart.
you must be convinced of
that.

i am.
i am pursuing the promise
the awakened bride.
it's not just revelation.
it's breath; it's life.
it's the awakening of my
senses for the very first
time.

i am my Beloved's & He
is mine.

"The Wooing"

"what do you see?",
he whispers.
such an intimate question.
almost an intrusion.
how dare you ask?
how dare you know about
the internal impression
that I didn't ask for…

i didn't say
I didn't honor it.
it's really not a violation.
it's more of a happening.
the kind of happening that
just happens when you're
so close to somebody.
close enough to know
what's on their mind.
what they're feeling.

"what do you see?",
he said.
"i see the bride dancing."
"dancing?"
"yeah, spinning wildly at
the altar."

he smiled.

- *"What Do You See?"*

shame is not aloud.
guilt is illegal.
transparency is not weak.
it's real.

it's on those days where
you just let yourself.
for no other reason than
you need to feel the
fullness of you.
it's okay to process.

those days where your
mind
is everywhere,
but within you.
& you feel the tear start to
fall because you can't
grasp the moment.

you know you aren't
present,
but you don't know
where you are either.

don't worry; He knows
about lament too.
He knows about
disappointment.
it's okay to feel.

it just allows you to
appreciate His whispers
a little more.
it lets you lean in a little
further.

"That's my girl."

- *"That's My Girl"*

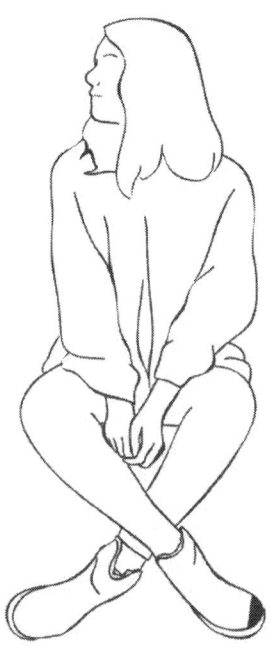

presentation is
everything.

positioned high, looking higher.
throwing my crown, because you are worth it.
you are set like nothing else.

who puts them back on?
casting over and over and over.
letting go of what wasn't mine to begin with.
giving back the very thing you sit before me.

only moving the same way you do.
that is honor.
imitation isn't flattery.
it's a privilege.

- ***"Presentation is Everything"***

our wedding
is no
secret.

- *"No More Secrets"*

delight
is the
difference.

- *"Delights of the Heart"*

i'm.
all.
yours.

- *"Whose?"*

"You're the best thing I
have ever waited for."

- *"The True Self"*

you are the object of my
affection.
how could I not honor
your longing?

if we are one,
how could you not feel
my breath?

if our eyes are locked,
my fire can't help but to
mark you.

this is one of a kind.
like you've never known.

I provide the oil.
I provide the fire.
you say yes.

this isn't about the doing.

your "yes" is your sound.

- ***"Response to
Affection"***

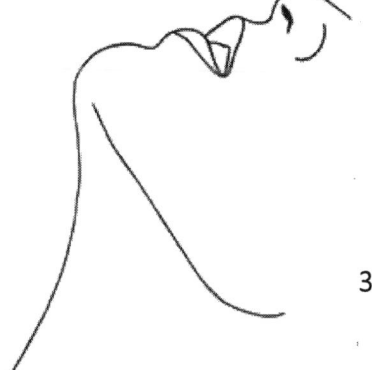

"i vow to steward this."
during encounter.
when father talks.
these are the words i whisper.
out loud. so it's real.
a response.

"i do."

i used to never think of your coming back as a good thing.
swept off.
death.
chaos.
gone.

loud trumpets.
mass destruction.
the glorious day we await.

it's not a reward.
it's a man coming to finish his wedding vows.

it's a husband visiting His wife.
it's the coming back for me.
not because I "accepted" You.
but because we were lovers.

- *"Vow to Steward"*

we made a good effort at
trying to tame what is.
it's just a
soft pull at the heart.
maybe a fast-paced beat.

"that's Him trying to tell
you something."

maybe your susceptibility
to emotional
inconsistency got you a
little teary-eyed.

how domesticated.

it's not the tug of a heart.
it's the person of God
trying to reveal Himself.
it's not a
simple bead of sweat.
it's the currency of
another realm that we are
unfamiliar with.

my internal world longs
to be struck with hits that
will conquer me.
strikes that don't have to
travel an unnecessary 18
inches,
but instead
penetrate the heart.
strikes that will change
everything.

i am positioned for
lightning.

- ***"Lightning Strikes"***

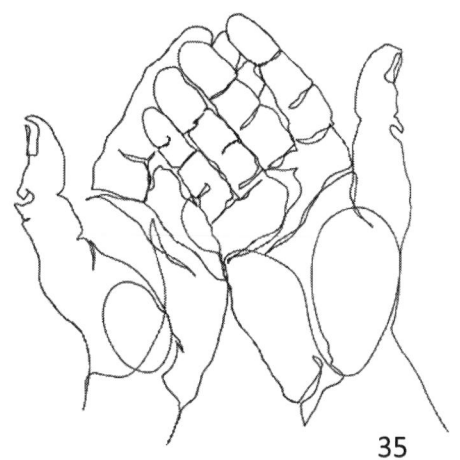

WHERE THE OIL WENT

Yahweh,
we know you are moving.
we can feel the wind.
we know you are excited
about the shifts.

you love to reveal the
deepest parts of your
heart to us.
we want to see.

you show the ones with
curious eyes.
to the ones who will keep
searching till they find it.
we honor those who have
found it.

bringing elucidation to
the world.
uncovering the secrets.
honor is the gateway to
strategy.
honor is the difference

we don't mind the
shaking.
do what you have to do.
you designed us for an
original intent.
& we vow to return to it.

so, we honor your heart.
we honor your plans.
we honor your promises.

- *"Curious Eyes"*

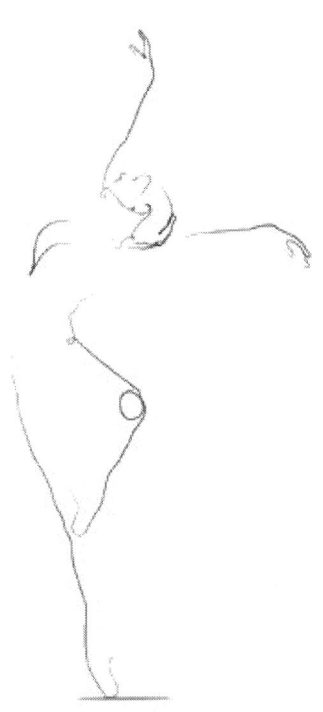

we are designed for
reproduction.
i think Hannah knew that.
more than that,
i think she knew how to do
it right.

she understood that what the
Lord gives
isn't hers to keep.
she already knew what a
double portion was.

*"If you give me what I have
asked, I will give it right
back."*

she was faithful
with her requests.
with her desires.
okay with accusation.

*"I am not drunk with wine.
I am drunk with intercession
to have a prophet."*

when fulfillment came
forth,
she had only one
explanation.

*"Because I asked the Lord
for him."*

if only we had the same
tenacity.
the same persistence to birth
the seed within.

my name is seed
& i am willing to be hidden.
to give myself right back.

we are not drunk with
compromise for temporary
fulfillment.
we are drunk with
intercession for what the
Lord is wanting to birth.

drunken babble it may be.
but it's my cry.
it's my promise.
it's my Samuel.

- ***"Hannah's Poem"***

our development starts
small.
no need to rush.
the process teaches how
to steward
what's been put inside of
us.

it's the hidden ones we
must learn to honor.
the vitals.
they are the ones created
and designed and
manifested in the secret
place.

the vitals.
the important parts.
we aren't permitted to be
seen until our insides
reach full development.
maturity.

what if we took time to be
carried?
nurtured?
sheltered?
attached to a life source.
unreliant on self.

we are part of a body.
often offering
our hands and feet,
but what if we said yes to
being an
internal extremity?
what if we found it
honorable to be in the
background?
giving allowance to
others.

- *"The Vitals"*

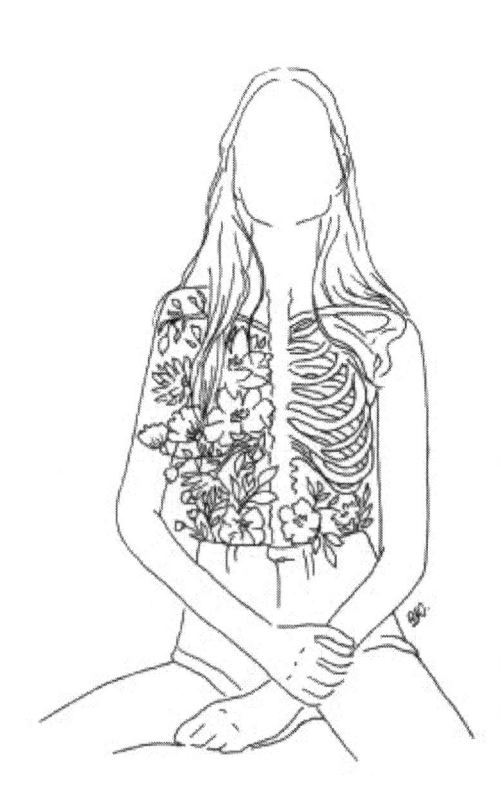

38

show us what it means to
live, Beloved.

the will of God is man
fully alive.
fully captivated by
presence.
by a man.

you don't wait for us to
get ready.
you just show up and
make an undeniable
invitation.
yes, the answer's yes.

that will be the answer
every time.
your bride is caught up in
a never ending "I do".

come build your territory
within us.
come teach us the
resurrected life.
show us what "in you"
feels like.

your dear one is excited
about the adventure that
awaits.

delight is the difference.
the delight of a glance.
the delight of a touch.
the delight of a voice.

show us what it means to
live, Beloved.

- *"How to Live"*

uncertainty
is part
of the adventure.

- *"Elements of Adventure"*

i vow
to become
Your wildest dreams.

- *"Destiny's Promise"*

i won't
become skeptical
with You
or Your promises.

- *"Skeptic"*

i want our life together
to be the greatest dance
i've ever known.

- *"Dance of Submission"*

i am a creative...
& not for the sake of art or showmanship
but because i have the ability to create new worlds within me
& the answer to the world around me is the world within me.

- *"The Creative"*

there are millions of words.
they are all at our disposal.
poetry is just knowing when, when not, and which ones.
it's all about choice,
but the beautiful thing is the Holy Spirit knows what He likes.

- *"Poetry"*

back and forth
we will sing,
from the bride to the King.
from the King to the bride,
there's no distance
between.

- *"No Distance"*

i am gloriously frustrated.
full of longing & yearning
& fire & passion.
hungry is what i am.
unapologetically hungry for
the glory that exuberates
from the most beautiful man.

it's a holy wonder.
it's a holy wild.
it's the adventure
of a lifetime.
it's the thrill of the unknown.

i am the one. i am the one.
i will climb Mount God.
the ascent… it's the ascent.
an ascended life, of an
awakened bride.
wildly running after her
groom.

He does not tease us.
He does not give us an
invitation that we can't
measure up to.

the pursuit is free,
but the cost is flesh.
that's okay, because i am
willing to give my
whole life.

if it's the only thing i have
left to give
i will give it all.

i don't know what it takes.
i don't know!
but I keep hearing the voice
whispering,
"there's more…",
"come up here…"

i am taking a stance of
no toleration.
a stance that says no to
everything else.

i will ascend
the Hill of the Lord!
I will wake up dreaming
of the will of God being
fulfilled in my life.

the will of God is man
fully alive.
and I am about to have the
time of my life.

- *"The Apostle"*

SAVANAH JUDD

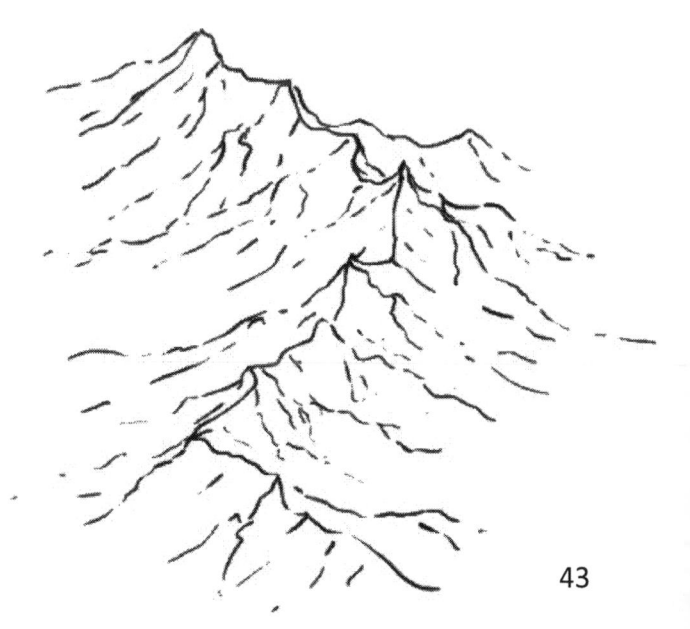

sinking deep into it all.
feeling the full weight of everything that comes at us.
we're all in,
not afraid of what's to come.

- *"All In"*

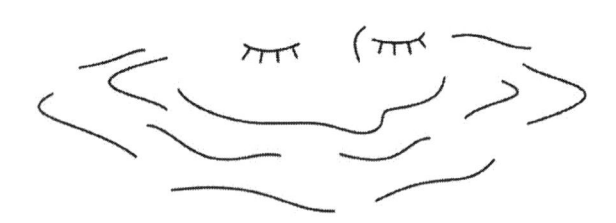

sometimes freedom isn't singing at the top of your lungs
or dancing like no one's watching.
sometimes it's not making a huge public announcement
that *"I'm free!"*.

sometimes it's taking thoughts captive;
it's choosing not to be overwhelmed,
even when you're being overwhelmed by EVERYTHING.

sometimes it's just breathing deep,
resting in identity and delight.
small moments hold the opportunity for freedom too.

- *"Freedom"*

i found a better way.
One with less staggering
& better view.
a way that leads and
never leaves
me wandering.
but if I do,
i'm lost in the right
direction.

the irresistible radiance.
the seductive abundance
of hope.
and i won't be scared of
hoping here.
here there is light.

& where there is light, i
am able to dance on my
disappointment.
just a little bit farther to
touch you.
in hopes to become one.
but for now I'll stay
within reach.
letting your rays wash
over me.

- *"Light"*

You are the perfect antidote.
the preventer
& the healer
& all the in between.

you're a trader.
joy for mourning,
beauty for ashes,
life for death,
freedom for bondage.

and you clothe me in the garment of praise.
You place on me what is light,
what is full of light
& You don't insult my heaviness,
You just make a better offer
& give me no other option than weightlessness.

You even offer me a footstool.
not just for my enemies,
but to help me ascend high above it all.
bringing new perspective,
breaking the barrier of bondage and releasing me into truth.
You're taking perfect care of me.
leading me in the way of the healed, the whole and the free.

- *"Antidote"*

i don't think you died just so we wouldn't have to,
but to show us how to go through
D E A T H
in such a way that it manifests a
R E S U R R E C T I O N.

i wonder what it would've been like in the grave.
were you a little groggy when you got up from your 3 day excursion?
did Your eyes have to adjust to the light
or were you so filled with it that there was no difference?
what was death like for the Son of Man?

what was your father feeling?
could You feel it too?
was He proud?

Your father gave His breath to give us life,
and You used Your last to do the same.
what a legacy.

the same tiny lungs that let heaven experience earth for the first time,
were the same lungs that let the
earth experience heaven for the first time.

i can only imagine the 33 years you lived
with skin and bone.
to know what was going on in the heaven
right inside of you.
to feel and know and hear the Father.

& you died and laid and got up so we could experience life
the way you did.
so, when mediocrity tries to avail
or the enemy tries to manipulate
it's just him trying to sew back the loose thread of the veil,
but what he forgets is that
you are a double-edged sword ready to break through time
and time again.
no more separation.

You just couldn't stay away.
resurrection wasn't enough.
so, you decided to share Your Spirit too.

"Did our hearts not burn within us?"
two millennia later and the fire's still going.

- "Did Our Hearts Not Burn?"

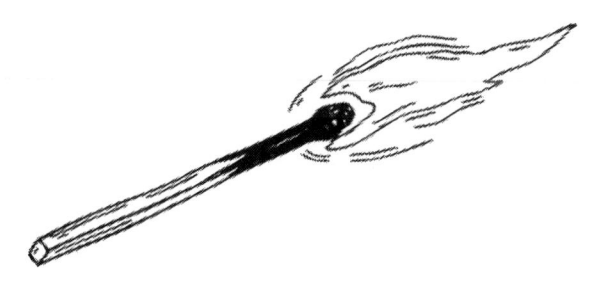

Here,
beneath me.
how I would love to build my life on intellect.
on certainty
on facts
on my own understanding,

but when the things that I know so
black and white
turn to gray,
the stack of books I have enthroned myself upon begin to topple
& the words on the pages begin to blur.

So, as much as I want to.
even if it contradicts everything I feel,
i will build my life on
Love
on the rock.
on the very thing that will keep me afloat when the rains beat and rise against me.
i will uproot myself in order to live.

- *"Beneath Me"*

SAVANAH JUDD

obedience is better than
sacrifice.
i don't know all that I'm
supposed to do.
i don't know how many
people and places and
things to accomplish.

how many hours of
sacrifice it takes.
or pleasures I have to
give up…
or disciplines i'm
supposed to partake in,
but i do know that
obedience is better than
sacrifice.

so, I will be obedient to
listen,
to stay close,
and to never look away.

- *"Better Than Sacrifice"*

the running may seem
beautiful.
the pace may seem
steady.
the form may look
just right.

but the runner is worth
nothing
if their lungs collapse
under the pressure of
performance
or their knees buckle
under the weight of the
world.

what are we even racing
for?
we're trying to play catch
up... but for what?

"Get ahead."
"Hurry up."
"You're running out of
time."

as if our zeal alone could
sustain us.
zeal alone
cannot sustain us.
passion cannot act as our
bread of life
& ambition cannot be the
cup we drink from.

if the pace isn't Jesus
if the vision isn't Jesus
if the standard isn't Jesus
then
i'm not running after it
because He is the only
vision of perfection I'm
chasing.

- *"The Chase"*

let the tears that stream down your cheeks
wash away the mask.
let the precious gift of vulnerability become your advocate
& let love be your shield.

let the fortress of your False self fade away
& the defenses stand down.
there's a temple full of intimacy waiting on the other side.

let the unveiling be full of grace
& beauty
& truth.

your life is worth more than warring with yourself.
self-preservation doesn't exist in this kingdom.
we made the exchange to receive foolishness.
we are free people.
"this is what freedom feels like…"

- *"The Mask"*

SAVANAH JUDD

let everything that is
be touched by creativity,

by the spirit, the cosmic force
that permeates all.

let everything that is
be touched by something more
that unlocks & unveils & renews.

everything that is
has been touched
& will flourish in its own way,
its own time

the Touch, which holds creativity,
set everything in motion
& it cannot be stopped

- *"Touched"*

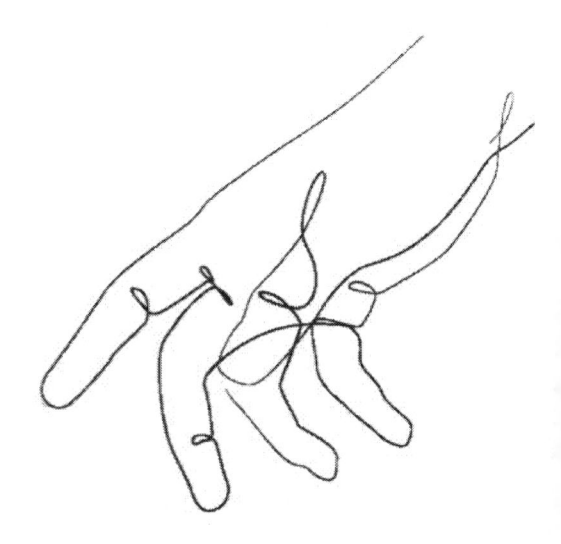

i sit and wait for the gaps to be filled in.
for my questions & curiosity,
not to shrink, but to expand.

it's not doubting;
it's creating capacity.

closure does not require itself to be rushed.
so, i don't have to rush towards it either.

i am on a search for truth.
that isn't wandering.
it's contemplation.

- *"Contemplation"*

"a Man of Suffering... acquainted with grief."

& what an acquaintance you are.
all too easy to become accompanied with.
so glib, inching your way closer and closer,
wrapping yourself around me,
seducing me deeper and deeper into your sorrows.

but because of this Man of Suffering,
i do not have to fornicate with such an acquaintance.
i can stay true & loyal
to the man
the Man of Suffering.

- *"The Acquaintance"*

SAVANAH JUDD

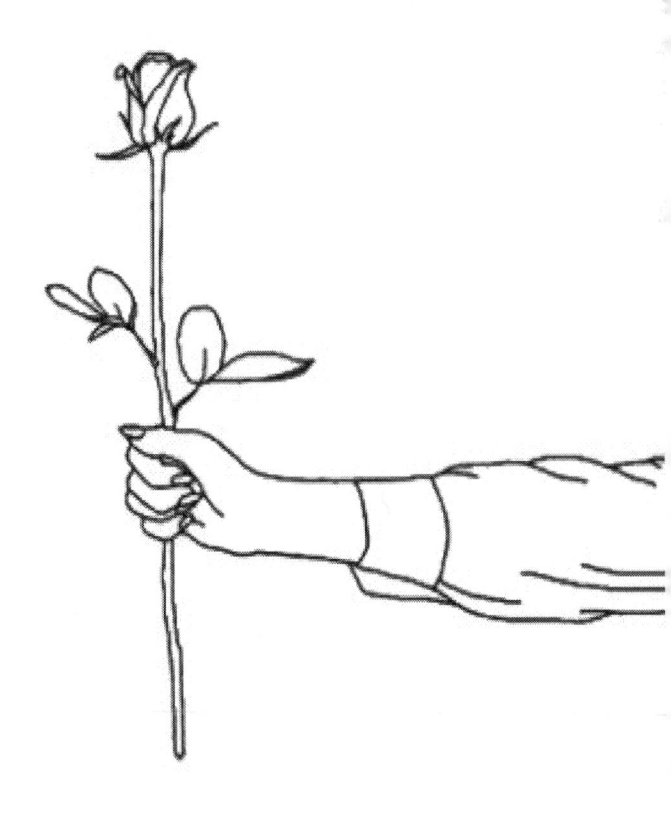

my introduction is pitiful & pathetic.
i stutter and stammer
& mistakenly downplay all that you are.

You are so hard to articulate.
One that cannot be formulated
or calculated.

You are so much better at being found,
 than i am at introducing You.

- *"My Intro"*

SAVANAH JUDD

mere humans.
let us come face to face with our humanity.
confront every part of it.

i don't think we were supposed to despise humanness.
God loves things by becoming them.
so, His great incarnation was us,
mere humans.

physicality & free will & sin.
all part of the human condition,
but the human condition is not
misery & disgust & despair.

the most beautiful human condition had
perfect pace
& deep relationships
& community.

the most beautiful human condition
was a close and tender friend.

the most beautiful human condition
was loving, joyful, peaceful, patient,
kind and good, disciplined.

& yet the one who was the epitome of
the human condition…
was a mere human.

- *"Mere Humans"*

dead & resurrected;
dying, yet being raised;
here & seated in heavenly places.
beautiful duality.

- *"Duality"*

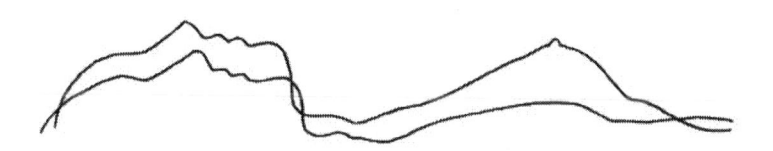

'til resurrection swallows me
- *"All of Me"*

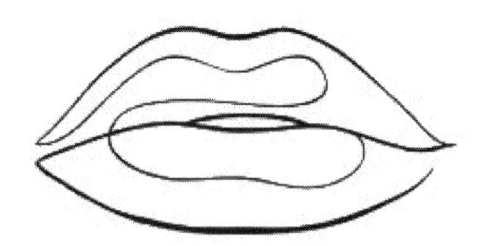

my pace could change the world,
could reset the clock,
could confront culture.

there is power in your name
& in your pace
& in the peace that You carry.

let me walk in that,
for it saves lives.

- *"Change of Pace"*

Rest is the forbidden pathway;
the ancient ruins we must rebuild.
peace is the treasure we must uncover
& refuse to trade.

the generations have been crying out for rest.

Rest looks like an outstretched arm.
maybe for the laying on of hands,
imparting gifts,
for the passing of the torch.
or maybe, just the simple act of surrender.

Rest is the exposure of all that is within us…
being laid into another.
Rest is the very thing that could save lives.

Rest is a promise I believe will be fulfilled.
not by our own doing,
but by our being.

and by being confident that the ones who come after us
will discover this pace,
will set us free from striving.

their momentum doesn't rely on us, but the hand of God.
that is rest.

- *"Rest"*

SAVANAH JUDD

I ended our time together with rest. Even through the exposing of pain and pouring oil on wounded places, without rest, none of it can be sustained. Rest is the most beautiful half of duality in the kingdom. We can be at rest and advancing. We can be at rest and creating. We can be at rest yet fighting for our lives at the same time. Rest is a truth that will never fade, like the Christ. He came to the earth and met it with the purest form of truth.

The Lord will ultimately come and reveal truth. always. Regardless of form or lack of form, in dream, whisper, shout, sensation, good, bad, pain, pleasure, person, nature, & even through our own hurting hearts…
He will come.
He will speak.

The voice of Truth brings clarity sharper than any double-edged sword.
Every word piercing and healing simultaneously.
And the listening. The listening is the glorious frustration we have the pleasure of experiencing.
This voice will change everything.

SAVANAH JUDD

Endnotes

* Not all images/illustrations used within this book are my own original work; they have been inspired by many incredible artists, some who remain unknown.
* While every poem is original, many were inspired by concepts and ideas from other men and women, some who are themselves authors, others I have the honor of calling friend and yet some who remain unknown.

Made in the USA
Columbia, SC
20 April 2020